KUMON MATH WORKBOOKS

Grade 1

Subtraction

Table of Numbers ◆1 to 100

Level ☆

Score
/100

Date / /

Name

1 Fill in the missing numbers.

25 points for completion

1	2	3	4	5	6	7	8	9	10
11									20
21	22	23	24	25	26	27	28	29	30
31									40
41	42	43	44	45	46	47	48	49	50

2 Fill in the missing numbers.

25 points for completion

51	52	53	54	55	56	57	58	59	60
61									70
71	72	73	74	75	76	77	78	79	80
81									90
91	92	93	94	95	96	97	98	99	100

③ Fill in the missing numbers.

25 points for completion

1									10
11	12	13	14	15	16	17	18	19	20
21									30
31	32	33	34	35	36	37	38	39	40
41									50

④ Fill in the missing numbers.

25 points for completion

51									60
61	62	63	64	65	66	67	68	69	70
71									80
81	82	83	84	85	86	87	88	89	90
91									100

When you finish the exercises, let's check your answers with your parents.

1 Fill in the missing numbers.

25 points for completion

1	2			5	6	7	8	9	10
11	12	13	14			17	18	19	20
21	22	23	24	25	26			29	30
31	32	33	34	35	36	37	38		
		43	44	45	46	47	48	49	50

2 Fill in the missing numbers.

25 points for completion

51	52	53	54			57	58	59	60
61	62	63	64	65	66			69	70
71	72	73	74	75	76	77	78		
		83	84	85	86	87	88	89	90
91	92			95	96	97	98	99	100

3 **Fill in the missing numbers.** 25 points for completion

1	2	3		5	6	7	8		10
11	12		14	15	16	17		19	20
21		23	24	25	26		28	29	30
	32	33	34	35		37	38	39	40
41	42	43	44		46	47	48	49	

4 **Fill in the missing numbers.** 25 points for completion

51	52	53	54		56	57	58	59	
	62	63	64	65		67	68	69	70
71		73	74	75	76		78	79	80
81	82		84	85	86	87		89	90
91	92	93		95	96	97	98		100

Did you check your answers?

5

1 Add.

2 points per question

(1) 6 + 1 =

(2) 5 + 1 =

(3) 7 + 1 =

(4) 3 + 1 =

(5) 4 + 1 =

(6) 2 + 1 =

(7) 8 + 1 =

(8) 9 + 1 =

(9) 2 + 2 =

(10) 3 + 2 =

(11) 5 + 2 =

(12) 7 + 2 =

(13) 9 + 2 =

(14) 4 + 2 =

(15) 6 + 2 =

(16) 8 + 2 =

(17) 5 + 3 =

(18) 4 + 3 =

(19) 1 + 3 =

(20) 3 + 3 =

(21) 7 + 3 =

(22) 8 + 3 =

(23) 2 + 3 =

(24) 6 + 3 =

(25) 9 + 3 =

2 Add.

(1) $8 + 1 =$

(2) $9 + 1 =$

(3) $6 + 2 =$

(4) $9 + 2 =$

(5) $8 + 3 =$

(6) $7 + 3 =$

(7) $7 + 2 =$

(8) $6 + 1 =$

(9) $6 + 3 =$

(10) $6 + 2 =$

(11) $5 + 1 =$

(12) $9 + 1 =$

(13) $9 + 3 =$

(14) $5 + 3 =$

(15) $5 + 2 =$

(16) $5 + 1 =$

(17) $8 + 3 =$

(18) $8 + 2 =$

(19) $4 + 3 =$

(20) $4 + 2 =$

(21) $3 + 1 =$

(22) $3 + 2 =$

(23) $3 + 3 =$

(24) $7 + 3 =$

(25) $7 + 2 =$

Did you remember your addition?

Review ◆ Adding 4 to Adding 6

Level

Date / /

Name

Score

/100

1 **Add.**

2 points per question

(1) $4 + 4 =$

(2) $2 + 4 =$

(3) $8 + 4 =$

(4) $9 + 4 =$

(5) $6 + 4 =$

(6) $5 + 4 =$

(7) $3 + 4 =$

(8) $7 + 4 =$

(9) $2 + 5 =$

(10) $1 + 5 =$

(11) $3 + 5 =$

(12) $5 + 5 =$

(13) $7 + 5 =$

(14) $9 + 5 =$

(15) $8 + 5 =$

(16) $6 + 5 =$

(17) $3 + 6 =$

(18) $1 + 6 =$

(19) $4 + 6 =$

(20) $2 + 6 =$

(21) $5 + 6 =$

(22) $8 + 6 =$

(23) $7 + 6 =$

(24) $6 + 6 =$

(25) $9 + 6 =$

2 Add.

(1) $5 + 4 =$

(2) $6 + 4 =$

(3) $3 + 5 =$

(4) $8 + 5 =$

(5) $2 + 6 =$

(6) $6 + 6 =$

(7) $7 + 5 =$

(8) $7 + 4 =$

(9) $9 + 5 =$

(10) $9 + 6 =$

(11) $9 + 4 =$

(12) $7 + 4 =$

(13) $7 + 6 =$

(14) $4 + 5 =$

(15) $4 + 6 =$

(16) $5 + 4 =$

(17) $5 + 5 =$

(18) $5 + 6 =$

(19) $3 + 5 =$

(20) $3 + 6 =$

(21) $8 + 4 =$

(22) $8 + 5 =$

(23) $8 + 6 =$

(24) $6 + 4 =$

(25) $6 + 5 =$

Good job! Don't forget to check your answers!

1 Add.

2 points per question

(1) $6 + 7 =$

(2) $2 + 7 =$

(3) $4 + 7 =$

(4) $7 + 7 =$

(5) $9 + 7 =$

(6) $8 + 7 =$

(7) $5 + 7 =$

(8) $3 + 7 =$

(9) $3 + 8 =$

(10) $6 + 8 =$

(11) $2 + 8 =$

(12) $1 + 8 =$

(13) $4 + 8 =$

(14) $5 + 8 =$

(15) $8 + 8 =$

(16) $7 + 8 =$

(17) $2 + 9 =$

(18) $4 + 9 =$

(19) $7 + 9 =$

(20) $9 + 9 =$

(21) $8 + 9 =$

(22) $3 + 9 =$

(23) $5 + 9 =$

(24) $5 + 0 =$

(25) $0 + 0 =$

2 Add.

(1) $5 + 7 =$

(2) $3 + 7 =$

(3) $4 + 8 =$

(4) $6 + 8 =$

(5) $4 + 9 =$

(6) $7 + 9 =$

(7) $7 + 8 =$

(8) $4 + 7 =$

(9) $4 + 8 =$

(10) $4 + 9 =$

(11) $5 + 7 =$

(12) $5 + 8 =$

(13) $5 + 9 =$

(14) $3 + 7 =$

(15) $3 + 8 =$

(16) $2 + 9 =$

(17) $1 + 8 =$

(18) $9 + 8 =$

(19) $5 + 0 =$

(20) $3 + 9 =$

(21) $2 + 8 =$

(22) $1 + 7 =$

(23) $6 + 7 =$

(24) $0 + 0 =$

(25) $9 + 9 =$

Are you ready to review counting and addition?

6 Addition Review

Date / /
Name

Level ☆☆

Score
/100

1 Fill in the missing numbers.

1 point per question

51		53	54	55	56		58	59	60
61	62	63		65	66	67	68		70
71	72	73		75			78	79	80
	82	83	84	85	86	87		89	90
91	92	93			96	97	98	99	

2 Add.

2 points per question

(1) 8 + 1 =

(2) 5 + 1 =

(3) 6 + 1 =

(4) 7 + 2 =

(5) 9 + 2 =

(6) 4 + 2 =

(7) 5 + 3 =

(8) 3 + 3 =

(9) 9 + 3 =

(10) 8 + 4 =

(11) 6 + 4 =

(12) 4 + 4 =

(13) 7 + 5 =

(14) 9 + 5 =

(15) 6 + 5 =

(16) 8 + 5 =

3 Add.

2 points per question

(1) $2 + 6 =$

(2) $5 + 6 =$

(3) $9 + 6 =$

(4) $4 + 7 =$

(5) $8 + 7 =$

(6) $6 + 7 =$

(7) $3 + 8 =$

(8) $5 + 8 =$

(9) $7 + 8 =$

(10) $4 + 9 =$

(11) $5 + 9 =$

(12) $8 + 9 =$

4 Add.

2 points per question

(1) $8 + 3 =$

(2) $7 + 3 =$

(3) $6 + 5 =$

(4) $9 + 6 =$

(5) $9 + 7 =$

(6) $8 + 5 =$

(7) $3 + 8 =$

(8) $3 + 9 =$

(9) $2 + 9 =$

(10) $9 + 4 =$

(11) $8 + 6 =$

(12) $7 + 4 =$

(13) $9 + 1 =$

(14) $9 + 9 =$

(15) $8 + 5 =$

(16) $4 + 0 =$

Great review! Now check your answers, and we can move on to subtraction!

Subtracting 1 ◆2−1 to 11−1

Date   /   /

Name

Score
/100

1 **Fill in the missing numbers.**

10 points for completion

1	2								

2 **Write each number while looking at the example above.**

11 points for completion

Example

10	9	8	7	6	5	4	3	2	1

3 **Fill in the missing numbers.**

5 points per question

(1)

10		8		6	5		3		1

(2)

10	9		7		

(5)

9		7		5	

(3)

8		6		4	

(6)

		6			3

(4)

6		4		2	

(7)

6					2

4 **Subtract while reading the number sentence aloud.**

2 points per question

1	2	3	4	5	6	7	8	9	10	11

(1) $2 - 1 = 1$
Two minus one equals one.

(2) $3 - 1 = 2$
Three minus one equals two.

(3) $4 - 1 = 3$

(4) $5 - 1 = 4$

(5) $6 - 1 =$

(6) $7 - 1 =$

(7) $8 - 1 =$

(8) $9 - 1 =$

(9) $10 - 1 =$

(10) $11 - 1 =$

5 **Subtract.**

2 points per question

(1) $2 - 1 =$

(2) $3 - 1 =$

(3) $5 - 1 =$

(4) $4 - 1 =$

(5) $7 - 1 =$

(6) $6 - 1 =$

(7) $8 - 1 =$

(8) $9 - 1 =$

(9) $10 - 1 =$

(10) $11 - 1 =$

(11) $3 - 1 =$

(12) $4 - 1 =$

If you are having trouble, try looking at the number line for a hint!

15

Date   /   /

Name

Score   /100

1 Subtract.

2 points per question

(1) 2 − 1 =

(2) 3 − 1 =

(3) 4 − 1 =

(4) 7 − 1 =

(5) 8 − 1 =

(6) 9 − 1 =

(7) 10 − 1 =

(8) 11 − 1 =

(9) 5 − 1 =

(10) 6 − 1 =

2 Subtract.

2 points per question

(1) 8 − 1 =

(2) 9 − 1 =

(3) 10 − 1 =

(4) 11 − 1 =

(5) 5 − 1 =

(6) 6 − 1 =

(7) 7 − 1 =

(8) 2 − 1 =

(9) 3 − 1 =

(10) 4 − 1 =

3 Subtract.

3 points per question

(1) $2 - 1 =$

(2) $4 - 1 =$

(3) $6 - 1 =$

(4) $8 - 1 =$

(5) $10 - 1 =$

(6) $3 - 1 =$

(7) $5 - 1 =$

(8) $7 - 1 =$

(9) $9 - 1 =$

(10) $11 - 1 =$

(11) $6 - 1 =$

(12) $8 - 1 =$

(13) $10 - 1 =$

(14) $5 - 1 =$

(15) $7 - 1 =$

(16) $9 - 1 =$

(17) $11 - 1 =$

(18) $4 - 1 =$

(19) $3 - 1 =$

(20) $5 - 1 =$

Subtraction can be difficult — good job!

9

Subtracting 1 ◆2−1 to 11−1

Level ★★

Date / /

Name

Score /100

1 **Subtract.**

2 points per question

(1) 6 − 1 =

(2) 8 − 1 =

(3) 10 − 1 =

(4) 5 − 1 =

(5) 7 − 1 =

(6) 9 − 1 =

(7) 11 − 1 =

(8) 7 − 1 =

(9) 5 − 1 =

(10) 3 − 1 =

2 **Subtract.**

2 points per question

(1) 4 − 1 =

(2) 3 − 1 =

(3) 2 − 1 =

(4) 11 − 1 =

(5) 10 − 1 =

(6) 9 − 1 =

(7) 8 − 1 =

(8) 7 − 1 =

(9) 6 − 1 =

(10) 5 − 1 =

3 Subtract.

(1) $4 - 1 =$

(2) $8 - 1 =$

(3) $3 - 1 =$

(4) $6 - 1 =$

(5) $11 - 1 =$

(6) $5 - 1 =$

(7) $10 - 1 =$

(8) $2 - 1 =$

(9) $4 - 1 =$

(10) $7 - 1 =$

(11) $9 - 1 =$

(12) $3 - 1 =$

(13) $5 - 1 =$

(14) $4 - 1 =$

(15) $2 - 1 =$

(16) $8 - 1 =$

(17) $7 - 1 =$

(18) $11 - 1 =$

(19) $10 - 1 =$

(20) $9 - 1 =$

You're doing really well. Keep it up!

1 **Fill in the missing numbers.** 10 points for completion

1	2												

2 **Write each number while looking at the example above.** 10 points for completion

Example

14	13	12	11	10	9	8	7	6	5	4	3	2	1

3 **Fill in the missing numbers.** 2 points per question

(1) | 14 | 13 | | 11 | | 9 |

(2) | 12 | | 10 | | 8 | |

(3) | | 9 | | | 6 | 5 |

(4) | 8 | | | 5 | | 3 |

(5) | | 5 | | 3 | 2 | |

(6) | 13 | | 11 | | 9 | 8 |

(7) | 11 | | | 8 | | 6 |

(8) | | 8 | 7 | | 5 | |

(9) | | 6 | | 4 | | 2 |

(10) | 6 | 5 | | 3 | | |

4 **Subtract.**

3 points per question

(1) $5 - 1 =$

(2) $6 - 1 =$

(3) $7 - 1 =$

(4) $8 - 1 =$

(5) $9 - 1 =$

(6) $10 - 1 =$

(7) $11 - 1 =$

(8) $12 - 1 =$

(9) $13 - 1 =$

(10) $14 - 1 =$

5 **Subtract.**

3 points per question

(1) $8 - 1 =$

(2) $9 - 1 =$

(3) $2 - 1 =$

(4) $3 - 1 =$

(5) $4 - 1 =$

(6) $12 - 1 =$

(7) $13 - 1 =$

(8) $14 - 1 =$

(9) $10 - 1 =$

(10) $11 - 1 =$

When you're finished, let's check your answers with your parents!

21

11

Subtracting 1 ◆2−1 to 14−1

Level ★★★

Date   /   /

Name

Score

/100

1 Subtract.

2 points per question

(1) 8 − 1 =

(2) 9 − 1 =

(3) 10 − 1 =

(4) 11 − 1 =

(5) 2 − 1 =

(6) 3 − 1 =

(7) 4 − 1 =

(8) 12 − 1 =

(9) 13 − 1 =

(10) 14 − 1 =

(11) 2 − 1 =

(12) 12 − 1 =

(13) 3 − 1 =

(14) 13 − 1 =

(15) 4 − 1 =

(16) 14 − 1 =

(17) 5 − 1 =

(18) 6 − 1 =

(19) 7 − 1 =

(20) 8 − 1 =

2 Subtract.

3 points per question

(1) $3 - 1 =$

(2) $7 - 1 =$

(3) $4 - 1 =$

(4) $8 - 1 =$

(5) $12 - 1 =$

(6) $5 - 1 =$

(7) $9 - 1 =$

(8) $13 - 1 =$

(9) $2 - 1 =$

(10) $11 - 1 =$

(11) $12 - 1 =$

(12) $9 - 1 =$

(13) $4 - 1 =$

(14) $11 - 1 =$

(15) $8 - 1 =$

(16) $3 - 1 =$

(17) $14 - 1 =$

(18) $10 - 1 =$

(19) $6 - 1 =$

(20) $13 - 1 =$

Have you mastered your −1 subtraction?

1 Subtract.

2 points per question

| 1 | 2 | 3 | 4 | 5 | 6 | 7 | 8 | 9 | 10 | 11 | 12 |

(1) $3 - 2 = 1$

(2) $4 - 2 = 2$

(3) $5 - 2 = 3$

(4) $6 - 2 = 4$

(5) $7 - 2 =$

(6) $8 - 2 =$

(7) $9 - 2 =$

(8) $10 - 2 =$

(9) $11 - 2 =$

(10) $12 - 2 =$

2 Subtract.

2 points per question

(1) $3 - 2 =$

(2) $4 - 2 =$

(3) $9 - 2 =$

(4) $8 - 2 =$

(5) $7 - 2 =$

(6) $10 - 2 =$

(7) $11 - 2 =$

(8) $12 - 2 =$

(9) $5 - 2 =$

(10) $6 - 2 =$

3 Subtract.

3 points per question

(1) $6 - 2 =$

(2) $7 - 2 =$

(3) $8 - 2 =$

(4) $9 - 2 =$

(5) $3 - 2 =$

(6) $4 - 2 =$

(7) $5 - 2 =$

(8) $10 - 2 =$

(9) $11 - 2 =$

(10) $12 - 2 =$

4 Subtract.

3 points per question

(1) $9 - 2 =$

(2) $10 - 2 =$

(3) $11 - 2 =$

(4) $12 - 2 =$

(5) $6 - 2 =$

(6) $7 - 2 =$

(7) $8 - 2 =$

(8) $3 - 2 =$

(9) $4 - 2 =$

(10) $5 - 2 =$

You can use the number line as a hint!
When you're done, let's check your score.

Level

Date / /

Name

Score
/100

1 Subtract.

2 points per question

(1) $3 - 2 =$

(2) $5 - 2 =$

(3) $7 - 2 =$

(4) $4 - 2 =$

(5) $6 - 2 =$

(6) $8 - 2 =$

(7) $10 - 2 =$

(8) $12 - 2 =$

(9) $9 - 2 =$

(10) $11 - 2 =$

2 Subtract.

2 points per question

(1) $5 - 2 =$

(2) $4 - 2 =$

(3) $3 - 2 =$

(4) $12 - 2 =$

(5) $11 - 2 =$

(6) $10 - 2 =$

(7) $9 - 2 =$

(8) $8 - 2 =$

(9) $7 - 2 =$

(10) $6 - 2 =$

3 **Subtract.**

(1) $3 - 2 =$

(2) $7 - 2 =$

(3) $4 - 2 =$

(4) $10 - 2 =$

(5) $9 - 2 =$

(6) $11 - 2 =$

(7) $12 - 2 =$

(8) $6 - 2 =$

(9) $4 - 2 =$

(10) $5 - 2 =$

(11) $6 - 2 =$

(12) $8 - 2 =$

(13) $3 - 2 =$

(14) $4 - 2 =$

(15) $12 - 2 =$

(16) $10 - 2 =$

(17) $6 - 2 =$

(18) $8 - 2 =$

(19) $9 - 2 =$

(20) $11 - 2 =$

Keep up the great work!

Level

Date   /   /

Name

Score
/100

1 Subtract.

2 points per question

(1) 6 − 2 =

(2) 7 − 2 =

(3) 8 − 2 =

(4) 9 − 2 =

(5) 10 − 2 =

(6) 11 − 2 =

(7) 12 − 2 =

(8) 13 − 2 =

(9) 14 − 2 =

(10) 15 − 2 =

2 Subtract.

2 points per question

(1) 9 − 2 =

(2) 10 − 2 =

(3) 3 − 2 =

(4) 4 − 2 =

(5) 5 − 2 =

(6) 13 − 2 =

(7) 14 − 2 =

(8) 15 − 2 =

(9) 11 − 2 =

(10) 12 − 2 =

3 Subtract.

(1) $4 - 2 =$

(2) $7 - 2 =$

(3) $10 - 2 =$

(4) $5 - 2 =$

(5) $8 - 2 =$

(6) $11 - 2 =$

(7) $6 - 2 =$

(8) $9 - 2 =$

(9) $14 - 2 =$

(10) $12 - 2 =$

(11) $13 - 2 =$

(12) $3 - 2 =$

(13) $15 - 2 =$

(14) $9 - 2 =$

(15) $14 - 2 =$

(16) $6 - 2 =$

(17) $12 - 2 =$

(18) $10 - 2 =$

(19) $8 - 2 =$

(20) $11 - 2 =$

Are you ready for −3 subtraction? Let's go!

1 **Subtract.**

2 points per question

| 1 | 2 | 3 | 4 | 5 | 6 | 7 | 8 | 9 | 10 | 11 | 12 | 13 |

(1) 4 − 3 = 1

(2) 5 − 3 = 2

(3) 6 − 3 =

(4) 7 − 3 =

(5) 8 − 3 =

(6) 9 − 3 =

(7) 10 − 3 =

(8) 11 − 3 =

(9) 12 − 3 =

(10) 13 − 3 =

2 **Subtract.**

2 points per question

(1) 4 − 3 =

(2) 5 − 3 =

(3) 10 − 3 =

(4) 9 − 3 =

(5) 8 − 3 =

(6) 11 − 3 =

(7) 12 − 3 =

(8) 13 − 3 =

(9) 6 − 3 =

(10) 7 − 3 =

3 Subtract.

3 points per question

(1) $7 - 3 =$

(2) $8 - 3 =$

(3) $9 - 3 =$

(4) $10 - 3 =$

(5) $4 - 3 =$

(6) $5 - 3 =$

(7) $6 - 3 =$

(8) $11 - 3 =$

(9) $12 - 3 =$

(10) $13 - 3 =$

4 Subtract.

3 points per question

(1) $10 - 3 =$

(2) $11 - 3 =$

(3) $12 - 3 =$

(4) $13 - 3 =$

(5) $7 - 3 =$

(6) $8 - 3 =$

(7) $9 - 3 =$

(8) $4 - 3 =$

(9) $5 - 3 =$

(10) $6 - 3 =$

I knew you could do it!
Let's practice some more!

Subtracting 3 ◆4−3 to 13−3

Date   /   /

Name

Score / 100

1 **Subtract.**

2 points per question

(1) $4 - 3 =$

(2) $6 - 3 =$

(3) $8 - 3 =$

(4) $5 - 3 =$

(5) $7 - 3 =$

(6) $9 - 3 =$

(7) $11 - 3 =$

(8) $13 - 3 =$

(9) $10 - 3 =$

(10) $12 - 3 =$

2 **Subtract.**

2 points per question

(1) $6 - 3 =$

(2) $5 - 3 =$

(3) $4 - 3 =$

(4) $13 - 3 =$

(5) $12 - 3 =$

(6) $11 - 3 =$

(7) $10 - 3 =$

(8) $9 - 3 =$

(9) $8 - 3 =$

(10) $7 - 3 =$

3 Subtract.

3 points per question

(1) 5 − 3 =

(2) 4 − 3 =

(3) 6 − 3 =

(4) 9 − 3 =

(5) 7 − 3 =

(6) 10 − 3 =

(7) 8 − 3 =

(8) 11 − 3 =

(9) 13 − 3 =

(10) 12 − 3 =

(11) 6 − 3 =

(12) 13 − 3 =

(13) 5 − 3 =

(14) 10 − 3 =

(15) 12 − 3 =

(16) 4 − 3 =

(17) 7 − 3 =

(18) 9 − 3 =

(19) 8 − 3 =

(20) 11 − 3 =

Have you mastered your −3 subtraction?

© Kumon Publishing Co., Ltd.   33

17

Subtracting 3 ◆3−3 to 16−3

Level ★★★

Date   /   /

Name

Score
        /100

1 **Subtract.**

2 points per question

(1) $7 - 3 =$

(2) $8 - 3 =$

(3) $9 - 3 =$

(4) $10 - 3 =$

(5) $11 - 3 =$

(6) $12 - 3 =$

(7) $13 - 3 =$

(8) $14 - 3 =$

(9) $15 - 3 =$

(10) $16 - 3 =$

2 **Subtract.**

2 points per question

(1) $10 - 3 =$

(2) $9 - 3 =$

(3) $4 - 3 =$

(4) $5 - 3 =$

(5) $6 - 3 =$

(6) $14 - 3 =$

(7) $15 - 3 =$

(8) $16 - 3 =$

(9) $12 - 3 =$

(10) $13 - 3 =$

3 Subtract.

(1) 7 − 3 =

(2) 10 − 3 =

(3) 4 − 3 =

(4) 6 − 3 =

(5) 8 − 3 =

(6) 11 − 3 =

(7) 5 − 3 =

(8) 12 − 3 =

(9) 9 − 3 =

(10) 13 − 3 =

(11) 6 − 3 =

(12) 8 − 3 =

(13) 14 − 3 =

(14) 16 − 3 =

(15) 10 − 3 =

(16) 7 − 3 =

(17) 15 − 3 =

(18) 13 − 3 =

(19) 4 − 3 =

(20) 3 − 3 = 0

A number minus itself always equals zero!

It's time for −4 subtraction!

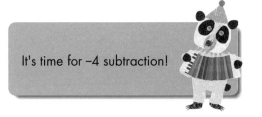

1   **Subtract.**

2 points per question

(1) $4 - 1 =$

(2) $4 - 2 =$

(3) $4 - 3 =$

(4) $5 - 1 =$

(5) $5 - 2 =$

(6) $5 - 3 =$

(7) $5 - 4 =$

(8) $6 - 1 =$

(9) $6 - 2 =$

(10) $6 - 3 =$

(11) $6 - 4 =$

(12) $7 - 2 =$

(13) $7 - 3 =$

(14) $7 - 4 =$

(15) $8 - 2 =$

(16) $8 - 3 =$

(17) $8 - 4 =$

(18) $10 - 2 =$

(19) $10 - 3 =$

(20) $10 - 4 =$

2 Subtract.

3 points per question

(1) $5 - 4 = 1$

(2) $6 - 4 = 2$

(3) $7 - 4 =$

(4) $8 - 4 =$

(5) $9 - 4 =$

(6) $10 - 4 =$

(7) $11 - 4 =$

(8) $12 - 4 =$

(9) $13 - 4 =$

(10) $14 - 4 =$

3 Subtract.

3 points per question

(1) $5 - 4 =$

(2) $6 - 4 =$

(3) $11 - 4 =$

(4) $10 - 4 =$

(5) $9 - 4 =$

(6) $12 - 4 =$

(7) $13 - 4 =$

(8) $14 - 4 =$

(9) $7 - 4 =$

(10) $8 - 4 =$

When you're done, don't forget to check your answers.

1 **Subtract.**   2 points per question

(1) $4 - 4 =$

(2) $6 - 4 =$

(3) $8 - 4 =$

(4) $10 - 4 =$

(5) $12 - 4 =$

(6) $5 - 4 =$

(7) $7 - 4 =$

(8) $9 - 4 =$

(9) $11 - 4 =$

(10) $13 - 4 =$

2 **Subtract.**   2 points per question

(1) $8 - 4 =$

(2) $5 - 4 =$

(3) $10 - 4 =$

(4) $9 - 4 =$

(5) $12 - 4 =$

(6) $7 - 4 =$

(7) $13 - 4 =$

(8) $11 - 4 =$

(9) $14 - 4 =$

(10) $6 - 4 =$

3 Subtract.

3 points per question

(1) $8 - 4 =$

(2) $9 - 4 =$

(3) $10 - 4 =$

(4) $11 - 4 =$

(5) $12 - 4 =$

(6) $13 - 4 =$

(7) $14 - 4 =$

(8) $15 - 4 =$

(9) $16 - 4 =$

(10) $17 - 4 =$

4 Subtract.

3 points per question

(1) $6 - 4 =$

(2) $9 - 4 =$

(3) $12 - 4 =$

(4) $15 - 4 =$

(5) $7 - 4 =$

(6) $10 - 4 =$

(7) $4 - 4 =$

(8) $8 - 4 =$

(9) $16 - 4 =$

(10) $11 - 4 =$

Have you mastered your −4 subtraction?

20

Subtracting 4 ◆4−4 to 17−4

Level ★★★

Date   /   /

Name

Score

/100

1 **Subtract.**

2 points per question

(1) $5 - 4 =$

(2) $4 - 4 =$

(3) $10 - 4 =$

(4) $17 - 4 =$

(5) $16 - 4 =$

(6) $11 - 4 =$

(7) $9 - 4 =$

(8) $12 - 4 =$

(9) $6 - 4 =$

(10) $13 - 4 =$

(11) $8 - 4 =$

(12) $7 - 4 =$

(13) $12 - 4 =$

(14) $15 - 4 =$

(15) $13 - 4 =$

(16) $10 - 4 =$

(17) $6 - 4 =$

(18) $14 - 4 =$

(19) $11 - 4 =$

(20) $16 - 4 =$

2 Subtract.

(1) $8 - 1 =$

(2) $5 - 1 =$

(3) $13 - 1 =$

(4) $9 - 1 =$

(5) $7 - 1 =$

(6) $9 - 2 =$

(7) $13 - 2 =$

(8) $7 - 2 =$

(9) $14 - 2 =$

(10) $10 - 2 =$

(11) $7 - 3 =$

(12) $9 - 3 =$

(13) $15 - 3 =$

(14) $10 - 3 =$

(15) $14 - 3 =$

(16) $9 - 4 =$

(17) $16 - 4 =$

(18) $11 - 4 =$

(19) $15 - 4 =$

(20) $12 - 4 =$

Are you ready to move on to −5 subtraction?

Subtracting 5 ◆6−5 to 15−5

Date   /   /

Name

Score   /100

1 Subtract.

2 points per question

(1) $6 - 2 =$

(2) $6 - 3 =$

(3) $6 - 4 =$

(4) $6 - 5 =$

(5) $7 - 2 =$

(6) $7 - 3 =$

(7) $7 - 4 =$

(8) $7 - 5 =$

(9) $8 - 2 =$

(10) $8 - 3 =$

(11) $8 - 4 =$

(12) $8 - 5 =$

(13) $9 - 2 =$

(14) $9 - 3 =$

(15) $9 - 4 =$

(16) $9 - 5 =$

(17) $10 - 2 =$

(18) $10 - 3 =$

(19) $10 - 4 =$

(20) $10 - 5 =$

2 Subtract.

3 points per question

(1) $6 - 5 = 1$

(2) $7 - 5 = 2$

(3) $8 - 5 =$

(4) $9 - 5 =$

(5) $10 - 5 =$

(6) $11 - 5 =$

(7) $12 - 5 =$

(8) $13 - 5 =$

(9) $14 - 5 =$

(10) $15 - 5 =$

3 Subtract.

3 points per question

(1) $6 - 5 =$

(2) $7 - 5 =$

(3) $12 - 5 =$

(4) $11 - 5 =$

(5) $10 - 5 =$

(6) $13 - 5 =$

(7) $14 - 5 =$

(8) $15 - 5 =$

(9) $9 - 5 =$

(10) $8 - 5 =$

When you're done, let's check your score!

1 **Subtract.**

2 points per question

(1) $5 - 5 =$

(2) $7 - 5 =$

(3) $9 - 5 =$

(4) $11 - 5 =$

(5) $13 - 5 =$

(6) $6 - 5 =$

(7) $8 - 5 =$

(8) $10 - 5 =$

(9) $12 - 5 =$

(10) $14 - 5 =$

2 **Subtract.**

2 points per question

(1) $8 - 5 =$

(2) $6 - 5 =$

(3) $14 - 5 =$

(4) $9 - 5 =$

(5) $11 - 5 =$

(6) $13 - 5 =$

(7) $7 - 5 =$

(8) $10 - 5 =$

(9) $15 - 5 =$

(10) $12 - 5 =$

3 Subtract.

3 points per question

(1) $9 - 5 =$

(2) $10 - 5 =$

(3) $11 - 5 =$

(4) $12 - 5 =$

(5) $13 - 5 =$

(6) $14 - 5 =$

(7) $15 - 5 =$

(8) $16 - 5 =$

(9) $17 - 5 =$

(10) $18 - 5 =$

4 Subtract.

3 points per question

(1) $7 - 5 =$

(2) $10 - 5 =$

(3) $14 - 5 =$

(4) $16 - 5 =$

(5) $8 - 5 =$

(6) $9 - 5 =$

(7) $6 - 5 =$

(8) $8 - 5 =$

(9) $18 - 5 =$

(10) $15 - 5 =$

Have you mastered your −5 subtraction?

1 **Subtract.**

2 points per question

(1) 7 − 5 =

(2) 11 − 5 =

(3) 6 − 5 =

(4) 16 − 5 =

(5) 12 − 5 =

(6) 8 − 5 =

(7) 10 − 5 =

(8) 15 − 5 =

(9) 17 − 5 =

(10) 14 − 5 =

(11) 16 − 5 =

(12) 17 − 5 =

(13) 13 − 5 =

(14) 9 − 5 =

(15) 18 − 5 =

(16) 5 − 5 =

(17) 14 − 5 =

(18) 11 − 5 =

(19) 8 − 5 =

(20) 12 − 5 =

2 Subtract.

3 points per question

(1) $7 - 1 =$

(2) $5 - 1 =$

(3) $11 - 1 =$

(4) $9 - 1 =$

(5) $4 - 2 =$

(6) $8 - 2 =$

(7) $14 - 2 =$

(8) $11 - 2 =$

(9) $5 - 3 =$

(10) $9 - 3 =$

(11) $12 - 3 =$

(12) $15 - 3 =$

(13) $8 - 4 =$

(14) $10 - 4 =$

(15) $13 - 4 =$

(16) $7 - 4 =$

(17) $9 - 5 =$

(18) $12 - 5 =$

(19) $16 - 5 =$

(20) $13 - 5 =$

You've made a lot of progress.
Keep up the good work!

1 **Subtract.**

2 points per question

(1) $5 - 2 =$

(2) $5 - 3 =$

(3) $5 - 4 =$

(4) $6 - 2 =$

(5) $6 - 3 =$

(6) $6 - 4 =$

(7) $6 - 5 =$

(8) $7 - 3 =$

(9) $7 - 4 =$

(10) $7 - 5 =$

2 **Subtract.**

2 points per question

(1) $7 - 2 =$

(2) $7 - 3 =$

(3) $7 - 4 =$

(4) $7 - 5 =$

(5) $7 - 6 =$

(6) $8 - 2 =$

(7) $8 - 3 =$

(8) $8 - 4 =$

(9) $8 - 5 =$

(10) $8 - 6 =$

3 Subtract.

3 points per question

(1) $9 - 2 =$

(2) $9 - 3 =$

(3) $9 - 4 =$

(4) $9 - 5 =$

(5) $9 - 6 =$

(6) $10 - 2 =$

(7) $10 - 3 =$

(8) $10 - 4 =$

(9) $10 - 5 =$

(10) $10 - 6 =$

4 Subtract.

3 points per question

(1) $7 - 4 =$

(2) $7 - 6 =$

(3) $8 - 4 =$

(4) $8 - 6 =$

(5) $8 - 5 =$

(6) $9 - 6 =$

(7) $9 - 3 =$

(8) $9 - 5 =$

(9) $10 - 6 =$

(10) $10 - 5 =$

Don't forget to show your parents how far you've come!

49

Subtraction

Date   /   /

Name

Level

Score /100

1 Subtract.

2 points per question

(1) $7 - 3 =$

(2) $7 - 5 =$

(3) $7 - 6 =$

(4) $7 - 4 =$

(5) $8 - 4 =$

(6) $8 - 3 =$

(7) $8 - 5 =$

(8) $8 - 6 =$

(9) $8 - 7 =$

(10) $9 - 3 =$

(11) $9 - 5 =$

(12) $9 - 4 =$

(13) $9 - 6 =$

(14) $9 - 7 =$

(15) $9 - 8 =$

(16) $10 - 5 =$

(17) $10 - 6 =$

(18) $10 - 7 =$

(19) $10 - 8 =$

(20) $10 - 9 =$

2 Subtract.

(1) $6 - 4 =$

(2) $6 - 6 =$

(3) $7 - 2 =$

(4) $7 - 5 =$

(5) $7 - 3 =$

(6) $7 - 6 =$

(7) $8 - 4 =$

(8) $8 - 3 =$

(9) $8 - 5 =$

(10) $8 - 6 =$

(11) $8 - 8 =$

(12) $9 - 8 =$

(13) $9 - 6 =$

(14) $9 - 7 =$

(15) $9 - 4 =$

(16) $10 - 2 =$

(17) $10 - 5 =$

(18) $10 - 7 =$

(19) $10 - 3 =$

(20) $10 - 6 =$

Have you mastered your −6 subtraction?

1 Subtract.

2 points per question

(1) 6 − 3 =

(2) 6 − 2 =

(3) 6 − 4 =

(4) 6 − 5 =

(5) 7 − 3 =

(6) 7 − 4 =

(7) 7 − 5 =

(8) 7 − 6 =

(9) 8 − 3 =

(10) 8 − 4 =

(11) 8 − 5 =

(12) 8 − 6 =

(13) 8 − 7 =

(14) 9 − 4 =

(15) 9 − 3 =

(16) 9 − 5 =

(17) 9 − 6 =

(18) 9 − 7 =

(19) 9 − 8 =

(20) 10 − 3 =

(21) 10 − 2 =

(22) 10 − 5 =

(23) 10 − 6 =

(24) 10 − 7 =

(25) 10 − 8 =

2 Subtract.

(1) $7 - 5 =$

(2) $7 - 7 =$

(3) $8 - 6 =$

(4) $8 - 7 =$

(5) $8 - 8 =$

(6) $9 - 5 =$

(7) $9 - 7 =$

(8) $9 - 9 =$

(9) $9 - 8 =$

(10) $10 - 6 =$

(11) $10 - 8 =$

(12) $10 - 10 =$

(13) $10 - 9 =$

(14) $9 - 3 =$

(15) $9 - 9 =$

(16) $9 - 6 =$

(17) $10 - 3 =$

(18) $10 - 7 =$

(19) $10 - 5 =$

(20) $10 - 4 =$

(21) $10 - 6 =$

(22) $10 - 2 =$

(23) $10 - 10 =$

(24) $10 - 8 =$

(25) $10 - 9 =$

You're doing really well!

Subtracting ◆From Numbers up to 11

Date / /

Name

Score /100

1 Subtract.

2 points per question

(1) $9 - 1 =$

(2) $10 - 1 =$

(3) $11 - 1 =$

(4) $10 - 2 =$

(5) $11 - 2 =$

(6) $10 - 3 =$

(7) $11 - 3 =$

(8) $10 - 4 =$

(9) $11 - 4 =$

(10) $9 - 5 =$

(11) $10 - 5 =$

(12) $11 - 5 =$

(13) $9 - 6 =$

(14) $10 - 6 =$

(15) $11 - 6 =$

(16) $9 - 7 =$

(17) $10 - 7 =$

(18) $11 - 7 =$

(19) $9 - 8 =$

(20) $10 - 8 =$

(21) $11 - 8 =$

(22) $10 - 9 =$

(23) $11 - 9 =$

(24) $10 - 10 =$

(25) $11 - 10 =$

2 Subtract.

2 points per question

(1) 9 − 3 =

(2) 10 − 3 =

(3) 11 − 3 =

(4) 10 − 5 =

(5) 11 − 5 =

(6) 9 − 7 =

(7) 10 − 7 =

(8) 11 − 7 =

(9) 9 − 9 =

(10) 10 − 9 =

(11) 11 − 9 =

(12) 10 − 10 =

(13) 11 − 11 =

(14) 10 − 4 =

(15) 10 − 7 =

(16) 11 − 5 =

(17) 11 − 8 =

(18) 11 − 2 =

(19) 11 − 6 =

(20) 11 − 9 =

(21) 11 − 4 =

(22) 11 − 7 =

(23) 11 − 3 =

(24) 11 − 11 =

(25) 11 − 10 =

When you're done, let's check your score!

28

Subtracting ◆From Numbers up to 12 ★★★

Level

Date / /

Name

Score

/100

1 Subtract.

2 points per question

(1) $10 - 1 =$

(2) $11 - 1 =$

(3) $12 - 1 =$

(4) $11 - 2 =$

(5) $12 - 2 =$

(6) $11 - 3 =$

(7) $12 - 3 =$

(8) $11 - 4 =$

(9) $12 - 4 =$

(10) $11 - 5 =$

(11) $12 - 5 =$

(12) $11 - 6 =$

(13) $12 - 6 =$

(14) $11 - 7 =$

(15) $12 - 7 =$

(16) $10 - 8 =$

(17) $11 - 8 =$

(18) $12 - 8 =$

(19) $10 - 9 =$

(20) $11 - 9 =$

(21) $12 - 9 =$

(22) $11 - 10 =$

(23) $12 - 10 =$

(24) $11 - 11 =$

(25) $12 - 11 =$

2 Subtract.

2 points per question

(1) $11 - 6 =$

(2) $12 - 6 =$

(3) $11 - 9 =$

(4) $12 - 9 =$

(5) $11 - 10 =$

(6) $12 - 10 =$

(7) $11 - 11 =$

(8) $12 - 11 =$

(9) $12 - 12 =$

(10) $12 - 0 = 12$

(11) $12 - 10 =$

(12) $11 - 11 =$

(13) $10 - 0 =$

(14) $12 - 2 =$

(15) $12 - 11 =$

(16) $12 - 8 =$

(17) $12 - 6 =$

(18) $12 - 3 =$

(19) $12 - 10 =$

(20) $12 - 4 =$

(21) $12 - 9 =$

(22) $12 - 12 =$

(23) $12 - 5 =$

(24) $12 - 1 =$

(25) $12 - 7 =$

Great work! Let's take another step forward!

Subtracting ◆From Numbers up to 13 ★★★

Level ★★★

Date / /

Name

Score

/100

1 **Subtract.**

2 points per question

(1) $10-1=$

(2) $13-1=$

(3) $10-2=$

(4) $13-2=$

(5) $10-3=$

(6) $13-3=$

(7) $10-4=$

(8) $13-4=$

(9) $10-5=$

(10) $13-5=$

(11) $10-6=$

(12) $13-6=$

(13) $11-7=$

(14) $13-7=$

(15) $12-8=$

(16) $13-8=$

(17) $12-9=$

(18) $13-9=$

(19) $12-10=$

(20) $13-10=$

(21) $12-11=$

(22) $13-11=$

(23) $12-12=$

(24) $13-12=$

(25) $13-13=$

2 Subtract.

(1) $11 - 3 =$

(2) $13 - 3 =$

(3) $11 - 5 =$

(4) $13 - 5 =$

(5) $11 - 8 =$

(6) $13 - 8 =$

(7) $11 - 9 =$

(8) $13 - 9 =$

(9) $11 - 11 =$

(10) $12 - 12 =$

(11) $12 - 0 =$

(12) $13 - 13 =$

(13) $13 - 0 =$

(14) $13 - 3 =$

(15) $13 - 6 =$

(16) $13 - 11 =$

(17) $13 - 8 =$

(18) $13 - 0 =$

(19) $13 - 7 =$

(20) $13 - 10 =$

(21) $13 - 5 =$

(22) $13 - 13 =$

(23) $13 - 4 =$

(24) $13 - 9 =$

(25) $13 - 12 =$

How are your subtraction skills?
Getting good, right?

1 Subtract.

2 points per question

(1) $10 - 1 =$

(2) $14 - 1 =$

(3) $10 - 2 =$

(4) $14 - 2 =$

(5) $10 - 3 =$

(6) $14 - 3 =$

(7) $10 - 4 =$

(8) $14 - 4 =$

(9) $10 - 5 =$

(10) $14 - 5 =$

(11) $10 - 6 =$

(12) $14 - 6 =$

(13) $10 - 7 =$

(14) $14 - 7 =$

(15) $10 - 8 =$

(16) $14 - 8 =$

(17) $10 - 9 =$

(18) $14 - 9 =$

(19) $10 - 10 =$

(20) $14 - 10 =$

(21) $12 - 11 =$

(22) $14 - 11 =$

(23) $12 - 12 =$

(24) $14 - 12 =$

(25) $14 - 13 =$

2 Subtract.

(1) $10 - 8 =$

(2) $11 - 8 =$

(3) $14 - 8 =$

(4) $11 - 9 =$

(5) $14 - 9 =$

(6) $11 - 11 =$

(7) $14 - 11 =$

(8) $13 - 12 =$

(9) $14 - 12 =$

(10) $13 - 13 =$

(11) $14 - 13 =$

(12) $14 - 14 =$

(13) $14 - 0 =$

(14) $14 - 2 =$

(15) $14 - 10 =$

(16) $14 - 3 =$

(17) $14 - 7 =$

(18) $14 - 4 =$

(19) $14 - 11 =$

(20) $14 - 8 =$

(21) $14 - 5 =$

(22) $14 - 0 =$

(23) $14 - 6 =$

(24) $14 - 9 =$

(25) $14 - 13 =$

Don't forget to check your answers when you're done!

1   **Subtract.**

2 points per question

(1) $10 - 1 =$

(2) $15 - 1 =$

(3) $10 - 2 =$

(4) $15 - 2 =$

(5) $10 - 3 =$

(6) $15 - 3 =$

(7) $10 - 4 =$

(8) $15 - 4 =$

(9) $10 - 5 =$

(10) $15 - 5 =$

(11) $10 - 6 =$

(12) $15 - 6 =$

(13) $10 - 7 =$

(14) $15 - 7 =$

(15) $12 - 8 =$

(16) $15 - 8 =$

(17) $12 - 9 =$

(18) $15 - 9 =$

(19) $12 - 10 =$

(20) $15 - 10 =$

(21) $12 - 11 =$

(22) $15 - 11 =$

(23) $14 - 12 =$

(24) $15 - 12 =$

(25) $15 - 13 =$

2 Subtract.

(1) 13 − 7 =

(2) 15 − 7 =

(3) 13 − 9 =

(4) 15 − 9 =

(5) 13 − 12 =

(6) 15 − 12 =

(7) 14 − 13 =

(8) 15 − 13 =

(9) 14 − 14 =

(10) 15 − 14 =

(11) 15 − 15 =

(12) 15 − 0 =

(13) 15 − 10 =

(14) 15 − 3 =

(15) 15 − 13 =

(16) 15 − 9 =

(17) 15 − 6 =

(18) 15 − 11 =

(19) 15 − 0 =

(20) 15 − 4 =

(21) 15 − 10 =

(22) 15 − 7 =

(23) 15 − 14 =

(24) 15 − 8 =

(25) 15 − 12 =

I knew you could do it! Let's try some more!

Subtracting ◆From Numbers up to 16 ★★★

Date / /

Name

Score

/100

1 Subtract.

2 points per question

(1) $12 - 6 =$

(2) $12 - 9 =$

(3) $12 - 10 =$

(4) $13 - 4 =$

(5) $13 - 7 =$

(6) $13 - 5 =$

(7) $13 - 9 =$

(8) $14 - 7 =$

(9) $14 - 3 =$

(10) $14 - 11 =$

(11) $14 - 5 =$

(12) $14 - 1 =$

(13) $14 - 12 =$

(14) $15 - 8 =$

(15) $15 - 13 =$

(16) $15 - 10 =$

(17) $15 - 9 =$

(18) $15 - 11 =$

(19) $15 - 12 =$

(20) $16 - 1 =$

(21) $16 - 2 =$

(22) $16 - 3 =$

(23) $16 - 4 =$

(24) $16 - 5 =$

(25) $16 - 6 =$

2 Subtract.

2 points per question

(1) $16 - 2 =$

(2) $16 - 4 =$

(3) $16 - 6 =$

(4) $16 - 7 =$

(5) $16 - 8 =$

(6) $16 - 9 =$

(7) $16 - 10 =$

(8) $16 - 12 =$

(9) $16 - 14 =$

(10) $16 - 16 =$

(11) $16 - 11 =$

(12) $16 - 13 =$

(13) $16 - 15 =$

(14) $16 - 10 =$

(15) $16 - 4 =$

(16) $16 - 12 =$

(17) $16 - 3 =$

(18) $16 - 13 =$

(19) $16 - 0 =$

(20) $16 - 16 =$

(21) $16 - 9 =$

(22) $16 - 5 =$

(23) $16 - 12 =$

(24) $16 - 8 =$

(25) $16 - 11 =$

You're getting really good! Let's take another step forward.

Subtracting ◆From Numbers up to 17

Level

Date / /

Name

Score

/100

1 Subtract.

2 points per question

(1) $12 - 4 =$

(2) $12 - 8 =$

(3) $13 - 6 =$

(4) $13 - 7 =$

(5) $14 - 6 =$

(6) $14 - 8 =$

(7) $15 - 5 =$

(8) $15 - 7 =$

(9) $15 - 9 =$

(10) $16 - 5 =$

(11) $16 - 8 =$

(12) $16 - 12 =$

(13) $16 - 14 =$

(14) $16 - 2 =$

(15) $16 - 3 =$

(16) $16 - 4 =$

(17) $16 - 7 =$

(18) $16 - 5 =$

(19) $17 - 3 =$

(20) $17 - 4 =$

(21) $17 - 5 =$

(22) $17 - 6 =$

(23) $17 - 7 =$

(24) $17 - 8 =$

(25) $17 - 9 =$

2 Subtract.

(1) $17 - 8 =$

(2) $17 - 6 =$

(3) $17 - 5 =$

(4) $17 - 7 =$

(5) $17 - 9 =$

(6) $17 - 11 =$

(7) $17 - 13 =$

(8) $17 - 15 =$

(9) $17 - 17 =$

(10) $17 - 10 =$

(11) $17 - 12 =$

(12) $17 - 14 =$

(13) $17 - 16 =$

(14) $17 - 7 =$

(15) $17 - 10 =$

(16) $17 - 6 =$

(17) $17 - 15 =$

(18) $17 - 11 =$

(19) $17 - 8 =$

(20) $17 - 14 =$

(21) $17 - 9 =$

(22) $17 - 12 =$

(23) $17 - 5 =$

(24) $17 - 17 =$

(25) $17 - 0 =$

If a problem looks tricky, just think about it a bit more!

## 34

Subtracting ◆From Numbers up to 18 ★★★

Level

Date   /   /

Name

Score

/100

1 **Subtract.**

2 points per question

(1) $14 - 8 =$

(2) $14 - 5 =$

(3) $14 - 12 =$

(4) $15 - 7 =$

(5) $15 - 10 =$

(6) $15 - 14 =$

(7) $15 - 6 =$

(8) $15 - 9 =$

(9) $16 - 2 =$

(10) $16 - 6 =$

(11) $16 - 11 =$

(12) $16 - 9 =$

(13) $16 - 16 =$

(14) $17 - 7 =$

(15) $17 - 12 =$

(16) $17 - 8 =$

(17) $17 - 14 =$

(18) $17 - 9 =$

(19) $18 - 3 =$

(20) $18 - 4 =$

(21) $18 - 5 =$

(22) $18 - 6 =$

(23) $18 - 7 =$

(24) $18 - 8 =$

(25) $18 - 9 =$

2 Subtract.

(1) $18 - 9 =$

(2) $18 - 7 =$

(3) $18 - 6 =$

(4) $18 - 8 =$

(5) $18 - 10 =$

(6) $18 - 12 =$

(7) $18 - 14 =$

(8) $18 - 16 =$

(9) $18 - 18 =$

(10) $18 - 11 =$

(11) $18 - 13 =$

(12) $18 - 15 =$

(13) $18 - 17 =$

(14) $18 - 6 =$

(15) $18 - 12 =$

(16) $18 - 4 =$

(17) $18 - 11 =$

(18) $18 - 14 =$

(19) $18 - 2 =$

(20) $18 - 13 =$

(21) $18 - 0 =$

(22) $18 - 9 =$

(23) $18 - 18 =$

(24) $18 - 1 =$

(25) $18 - 17 =$

These may seem like big numbers, but you can do it!

## 35

Subtracting ◆From Numbers up to 19

Level ★★★

Date   /   /

Name

Score /100

1 Subtract.

2 points per question

(1) 14 − 4 =

(2) 14 − 11 =

(3) 15 − 6 =

(4) 15 − 9 =

(5) 16 − 12 =

(6) 16 − 14 =

(7) 16 − 9 =

(8) 17 − 10 =

(9) 17 − 16 =

(10) 17 − 13 =

(11) 18 − 9 =

(12) 18 − 15 =

(13) 18 − 5 =

(14) 18 − 8 =

(15) 18 − 14 =

(16) 18 − 9 =

(17) 18 − 11 =

(18) 18 − 16 =

(19) 19 − 3 =

(20) 19 − 4 =

(21) 19 − 5 =

(22) 19 − 6 =

(23) 19 − 7 =

(24) 19 − 8 =

(25) 19 − 9 =

2 Subtract.

(1) $19 - 8 =$

(2) $19 - 4 =$

(3) $19 - 9 =$

(4) $19 - 10 =$

(5) $19 - 11 =$

(6) $19 - 13 =$

(7) $19 - 15 =$

(8) $19 - 12 =$

(9) $19 - 14 =$

(10) $19 - 16 =$

(11) $19 - 18 =$

(12) $19 - 17 =$

(13) $19 - 19 =$

(14) $19 - 10 =$

(15) $19 - 15 =$

(16) $19 - 7 =$

(17) $19 - 3 =$

(18) $19 - 9 =$

(19) $19 - 2 =$

(20) $19 - 11 =$

(21) $19 - 14 =$

(22) $19 - 17 =$

(23) $19 - 12 =$

(24) $19 - 1 =$

(25) $19 - 18 =$

Nicely done! Now let's take on the 20's!

Subtracting ◆From Numbers up to 20 ★★★

Level

Date   /   /

Name

Score

/100

1 Subtract.

2 points per question

(1) 16−11=

(2) 16− 8 =

(3) 16− 6 =

(4) 17− 9 =

(5) 17−11=

(6) 17− 8 =

(7) 18−13=

(8) 18− 9 =

(9) 18− 5 =

(10) 18−15=

(11) 19−10=

(12) 19−16=

(13) 19− 9 =

(14) 19−14=

(15) 19−17=

(16) 20− 1 =

(17) 20− 2 =

(18) 20− 3 =

(19) 20− 4 =

(20) 20− 5 =

(21) 20− 6 =

(22) 20− 7 =

(23) 20− 8 =

(24) 20− 9 =

(25) 20−10=

2 Subtract.

2 points per question

(1) 20 − 5 =

(2) 20 − 15 =

(3) 20 − 4 =

(4) 20 − 14 =

(5) 20 − 6 =

(6) 20 − 16 =

(7) 20 − 7 =

(8) 20 − 17 =

(9) 20 − 9 =

(10) 20 − 19 =

(11) 20 − 8 =

(12) 20 − 18 =

(13) 20 − 1 =

(14) 20 − 11 =

(15) 20 − 3 =

(16) 20 − 13 =

(17) 20 − 2 =

(18) 20 − 12 =

(19) 20 − 10 =

(20) 20 − 20 =

(21) 20 − 0 =

(22) 19 − 19 =

(23) 19 − 0 =

(24) 18 − 12 =

(25) 0 − 0 = 0

(25) Nothing minus nothing equals zero.

You did it! Now let's try a little bit of everything.

73

Date
/   /

Name

Score
/100

1 Subtract.

2 points per question

(1) 5 − 3 =

(2) 12 − 1 =

(3) 6 − 6 =

(4) 9 − 3 =

(5) 19 − 13 =

(6) 19 − 15 =

(7) 11 − 10 =

(8) 14 − 6 =

(9) 18 − 16 =

(10) 20 − 19 =

(11) 15 − 14 =

(12) 16 − 5 =

(13) 8 − 3 =

(14) 10 − 8 =

(15) 20 − 18 =

(16) 19 − 17 =

(17) 17 − 3 =

(18) 6 − 5 =

(19) 3 − 1 =

(20) 13 − 7 =

(21) 14 − 9 =

(22) 12 − 11 =

(23) 20 − 12 =

(24) 18 − 6 =

(25) 15 − 7 =

2 Subtract.

(1) $18-15=$

(2) $15-13=$

(3) $19-14=$

(4) $20-8=$

(5) $13-9=$

(6) $19-10=$

(7) $18-1=$

(8) $8-2=$

(9) $20-4=$

(10) $7-3=$

(11) $20-5=$

(12) $19-16=$

(13) $14-0=$

(14) $19-17=$

(15) $20-19=$

(16) $16-8=$

(17) $20-20=$

(18) $11-4=$

(19) $14-10=$

(20) $9-5=$

(21) $19-15=$

(22) $15-7=$

(23) $18-16=$

(24) $10-6=$

(25) $15-8=$

Did you remember everything you learned?

1 Subtract.

2 points per question

(1) $17 - 9 =$

(2) $18 - 8 =$

(3) $19 - 3 =$

(4) $10 - 1 =$

(5) $11 - 3 =$

(6) $12 - 5 =$

(7) $20 - 8 =$

(8) $16 - 12 =$

(9) $13 - 9 =$

(10) $15 - 14 =$

(11) $19 - 7 =$

(12) $11 - 4 =$

(13) $14 - 10 =$

(14) $9 - 5 =$

(15) $19 - 15 =$

(16) $15 - 7 =$

(17) $18 - 16 =$

(18) $10 - 6 =$

(19) $15 - 8 =$

(20) $17 - 9 =$

(21) $18 - 8 =$

(22) $19 - 3 =$

(23) $12 - 2 =$

(24) $16 - 7 =$

(25) $7 - 5 =$

2 Subtract.

(1) $13 - 3 =$

(2) $17 - 15 =$

(3) $15 - 11 =$

(4) $18 - 6 =$

(5) $20 - 15 =$

(6) $12 - 6 =$

(7) $14 - 7 =$

(8) $16 - 3 =$

(9) $18 - 9 =$

(10) $8 - 4 =$

(11) $15 - 10 =$

(12) $20 - 12 =$

(13) $10 - 2 =$

(14) $14 - 4 =$

(15) $17 - 6 =$

(16) $20 - 7 =$

(17) $8 - 4 =$

(18) $17 - 3 =$

(19) $15 - 4 =$

(20) $19 - 5 =$

(21) $20 - 8 =$

(22) $19 - 14 =$

(23) $16 - 7 =$

(24) $19 - 5 =$

(25) $20 - 2 =$

Don't forget to check your score!

Subtraction Review

39

Level ★★★

Date / /

Name

Score /100

1 Subtract.

2 points per question

(1) 19 − 3 =

(2) 16 − 9 =

(3) 19 − 8 =

(4) 18 − 9 =

(5) 19 − 6 =

(6) 9 − 3 =

(7) 17 − 10 =

(8) 16 − 11 =

(9) 18 − 8 =

(10) 15 − 11 =

(11) 7 − 5 =

(12) 19 − 12 =

(13) 20 − 14 =

(14) 18 − 6 =

(15) 20 − 9 =

(16) 15 − 8 =

(17) 18 − 12 =

(18) 20 − 3 =

(19) 18 − 15 =

(20) 17 − 4 =

(21) 20 − 6 =

(22) 17 − 9 =

(23) 18 − 4 =

(24) 19 − 18 =

(25) 17 − 15 =

2 Subtract.

(1) $20 - 10 =$

(2) $17 - 2 =$

(3) $13 - 4 =$

(4) $14 - 9 =$

(5) $19 - 17 =$

(6) $11 - 8 =$

(7) $20 - 11 =$

(8) $18 - 5 =$

(9) $14 - 11 =$

(10) $15 - 7 =$

(11) $18 - 13 =$

(12) $12 - 6 =$

(13) $16 - 10 =$

(14) $19 - 16 =$

(15) $20 - 2 =$

(16) $9 - 4 =$

(17) $12 - 8 =$

(18) $10 - 5 =$

(19) $16 - 13 =$

(20) $20 - 15 =$

(21) $11 - 7 =$

(22) $8 - 6 =$

(23) $14 - 7 =$

(24) $16 - 8 =$

(25) $20 - 13 =$

Are you ready to learn something new?

Three One-Digit Numbers

## 40

◆Mixed Calculations

Level ★★★

Date   /   /

Name

Score   / 100

1   Add.

2 points per question

(1) $2 + 1 + 3 = 6$

(2) $3 + 1 + 4 =$

(3) $3 + 6 + 1 =$

(4) $4 + 1 + 2 =$

(5) $4 + 4 + 2 =$

(6) $5 + 1 + 3 =$

(7) $5 + 3 + 2 =$

(8) $6 + 1 + 3 =$

(9) $6 + 4 + 3 =$

(10) $7 + 3 + 2 =$

2   Subtract.

2 points per question

(1) $9 - 1 - 5 = 3$

(2) $6 - 2 - 1 =$

(3) $7 - 3 - 1 =$

(4) $8 - 2 - 4 =$

(5) $9 - 3 - 2 =$

(6) $9 - 4 - 1 =$

(7) $10 - 4 - 2 =$

(8) $10 - 5 - 3 =$

(9) $12 - 2 - 1 =$

(10) $14 - 4 - 2 =$

3 Add and subtract.

3 points per question

(1) $3 + 1 + 5 =$

(2) $2 + 4 + 1 =$

(3) $4 + 3 + 2 =$

(4) $5 + 2 + 2 =$

(5) $7 + 3 + 1 =$

(6) $4 + 1 + 2 =$

(7) $6 + 4 + 4 =$

(8) $5 + 1 + 4 =$

(9) $3 + 2 + 5 =$

(10) $9 + 1 + 2 =$

(11) $8 - 1 - 2 =$

(12) $6 - 3 - 1 =$

(13) $9 - 1 - 4 =$

(14) $11 - 1 - 3 =$

(15) $12 - 2 - 4 =$

(16) $6 - 4 - 1 =$

(17) $8 - 3 - 2 =$

(18) $10 - 6 - 3 =$

(19) $9 - 5 - 1 =$

(20) $14 - 4 - 3 =$

Remember, just take it step by step!
You're doing fine!

81

41

◆Mixed Calculations

Level ★★★

Date / /

Name

Score /100

1 Calculate.

2 points per question

(1) $4 + 3 - 1 = 6$

(2) $4 + 6 - 7 =$

(3) $5 + 2 - 4 =$

(4) $5 + 4 - 8 =$

(5) $6 + 1 - 2 =$

(6) $6 + 3 - 5 =$

(7) $7 + 3 - 4 =$

(8) $7 + 4 - 6 =$

(9) $8 + 2 - 3 =$

(10) $8 + 4 - 7 =$

2 Calculate.

2 points per question

(1) $5 - 1 + 2 = 6$

(2) $6 - 4 + 1 =$

(3) $8 - 4 + 1 =$

(4) $8 - 5 + 3 =$

(5) $9 - 3 + 2 =$

(6) $9 - 6 + 5 =$

(7) $10 - 8 + 6 =$

(8) $10 - 4 + 2 =$

(9) $11 - 4 + 2 =$

(10) $11 - 3 + 4 =$

© Kumon Publishing Co., Ltd.

3 Calculate.

3 points per question

(1) $5 + 3 - 7 =$

(2) $7 + 2 - 6 =$

(3) $4 + 6 - 5 =$

(4) $6 + 5 - 1 =$

(5) $2 + 8 - 4 =$

(6) $3 + 6 - 7 =$

(7) $5 + 4 - 2 =$

(8) $8 + 3 - 5 =$

(9) $6 + 4 - 9 =$

(10) $4 + 9 - 6 =$

(11) $6 - 1 + 3 =$

(12) $9 - 5 + 2 =$

(13) $7 - 6 + 4 =$

(14) $4 - 2 + 5 =$

(15) $10 - 4 + 3 =$

(16) $12 - 7 + 6 =$

(17) $5 - 3 + 4 =$

(18) $7 - 4 + 5 =$

(19) $11 - 2 + 1 =$

(20) $13 - 5 + 4 =$

Great! Now let's check your score!

Three One-Digit Numbers
◆Mixed Calculations

42

Level

Score

Date / /

Name

/100

1 Calculate.

2 points per question

(1) $2 + 1 + 4 =$

(2) $3 + 7 + 1 =$

(3) $5 + 2 + 5 =$

(4) $9 - 2 - 4 =$

(5) $6 - 1 - 3 =$

(6) $7 - 2 - 3 =$

(7) $4 + 4 - 2 =$

(8) $5 + 1 - 3 =$

(9) $7 + 2 - 3 =$

(10) $5 - 2 + 3 =$

(11) $8 - 3 + 2 =$

(12) $9 - 4 + 3 =$

(13) $4 + 2 + 3 =$

(14) $9 - 2 - 5 =$

(15) $2 + 7 - 3 =$

(16) $7 - 5 + 3 =$

(17) $6 + 3 + 3 =$

(18) $9 - 4 - 2 =$

(19) $8 + 2 - 4 =$

(20) $7 - 3 + 4 =$

2 Calculate.

3 points per question

(1) $6 + 4 + 3 =$

(2) $9 + 1 + 3 =$

(3) $10 - 5 - 2 =$

(4) $11 - 1 - 5 =$

(5) $6 + 4 - 7 =$

(6) $3 + 7 - 5 =$

(7) $10 - 5 + 4 =$

(8) $11 - 3 + 1 =$

(9) $7 + 3 + 3 =$

(10) $14 - 4 - 5 =$

(11) $8 + 4 - 6 =$

(12) $12 - 6 + 7 =$

(13) $5 + 8 - 6 =$

(14) $9 - 3 - 2 =$

(15) $11 - 4 + 2 =$

(16) $8 + 2 + 5 =$

(17) $12 - 6 - 3 =$

(18) $7 + 6 - 8 =$

(19) $10 - 5 + 4 =$

(20) $8 + 5 - 6 =$

Are you ready to review what you've learned?

Review

Date / /

Name

Level ★★★

Score /100

1 **Subtract.**

2 points per question

(1) $6 - 3 =$

(2) $8 - 5 =$

(3) $11 - 4 =$

(4) $9 - 3 =$

(5) $4 - 1 =$

(6) $3 - 3 =$

(7) $7 - 2 =$

(8) $13 - 5 =$

(9) $10 - 1 =$

(10) $8 - 4 =$

(11) $5 - 3 =$

(12) $7 - 2 =$

(13) $9 - 5 =$

(14) $11 - 2 =$

(15) $14 - 5 =$

(16) $9 - 1 =$

(17) $5 - 5 =$

(18) $6 - 4 =$

(19) $8 - 3 =$

(20) $3 - 2 =$

(21) $7 - 3 =$

(22) $4 - 0 =$

(23) $8 - 5 =$

(24) $10 - 4 =$

(25) $12 - 3 =$

2 Subtract.

(1) $10-6=$

(2) $12-8=$

(3) $9-7=$

(4) $11-5=$

(5) $14-9=$

(6) $8-6=$

(7) $10-4=$

(8) $15-7=$

(9) $13-8=$

(10) $18-9=$

(11) $16-7=$

(12) $10-5=$

(13) $7-6=$

(14) $9-5=$

(15) $14-7=$

(16) $10-8=$

(17) $15-9=$

(18) $11-3=$

(19) $12-6=$

(20) $8-8=$

(21) $10-7=$

(22) $17-8=$

(23) $14-5=$

(24) $16-7=$

(25) $11-9=$

Conglatulations! You are ready for *Grade 2 Addition*!

1 **Table of Numbers** ◆1 to 100   pp 2, 3

1
1	2	3	4	5	6	7	8	9	10
11	12	13	14	15	16	17	18	19	20
21	22	23	24	25	26	27	28	29	30
31	32	33	34	35	36	37	38	39	40
41	42	43	44	45	46	47	48	49	50

2
51	52	53	54	55	56	57	58	59	60
61	62	63	64	65	66	67	68	69	70
71	72	73	74	75	76	77	78	79	80
81	82	83	84	85	86	87	88	89	90
91	92	93	94	95	96	97	98	99	100

3
1	2	3	4	5	6	7	8	9	10
11	12	13	14	15	16	17	18	19	20
21	22	23	24	25	26	27	28	29	30
31	32	33	34	35	36	37	38	39	40
41	42	43	44	45	46	47	48	49	50

4
51	52	53	54	55	56	57	58	59	60
61	62	63	64	65	66	67	68	69	70
71	72	73	74	75	76	77	78	79	80
81	82	83	84	85	86	87	88	89	90
91	92	93	94	95	96	97	98	99	100

2 **Table of Numbers** ◆1 to 100   pp 4, 5

1
1	2	3	4	5	6	7	8	9	10
11	12	13	14	15	16	17	18	19	20
21	22	23	24	25	26	27	28	29	30
31	32	33	34	35	36	37	38	39	40
41	42	43	44	45	46	47	48	49	50

2
51	52	53	54	55	56	57	58	59	60
61	62	63	64	65	66	67	68	69	70
71	72	73	74	75	76	77	78	79	80
81	82	83	84	85	86	87	88	89	90
91	92	93	94	95	96	97	98	99	100

3
1	2	3	4	5	6	7	8	9	10
11	12	13	14	15	16	17	18	19	20
21	22	23	24	25	26	27	28	29	30
31	32	33	34	35	36	37	38	39	40
41	42	43	44	45	46	47	48	49	50

4
51	52	53	54	55	56	57	58	59	60
61	62	63	64	65	66	67	68	69	70
71	72	73	74	75	76	77	78	79	80
81	82	83	84	85	86	87	88	89	90
91	92	93	94	95	96	97	98	99	100

Advice

Do you remember all of your numbers from 1 to 100? If not, try practicing them some more.

3 **Review** ◆Adding 1 to Adding 3   pp 6, 7

1
(1) 7	(14) 6
(2) 6	(15) 8
(3) 8	(16) 10
(4) 4	(17) 8
(5) 5	(18) 7
(6) 3	(19) 4
(7) 9	(20) 6
(8) 10	(21) 10
(9) 4	(22) 11
(10) 5	(23) 5
(11) 7	(24) 9
(12) 9	(25) 12
(13) 11	

2
(1) 9	(14) 8
(2) 10	(15) 7
(3) 8	(16) 6
(4) 11	(17) 11
(5) 11	(18) 10
(6) 10	(19) 7
(7) 9	(20) 6
(8) 7	(21) 4
(9) 9	(22) 5
(10) 8	(23) 6
(11) 6	(24) 10
(12) 10	(25) 9
(13) 12	

4 Review ◆Adding 4 to Adding 6 · pp 8,9

1

(1) 8		(14) 14	
(2) 6		(15) 13	
(3) 12		(16) 11	
(4) 13		(17) 9	
(5) 10		(18) 7	
(6) 9		(19) 10	
(7) 7		(20) 8	
(8) 11		(21) 11	
(9) 7		(22) 14	
(10) 6		(23) 13	
(11) 8		(24) 12	
(12) 10		(25) 15	
(13) 12			

2

(1) 9		(14) 9	
(2) 10		(15) 10	
(3) 8		(16) 9	
(4) 13		(17) 10	
(5) 8		(18) 11	
(6) 12		(19) 8	
(7) 12		(20) 9	
(8) 11		(21) 12	
(9) 14		(22) 13	
(10) 15		(23) 14	
(11) 13		(24) 10	
(12) 11		(25) 11	
(13) 13			

2

(1) 9		(9) 12	
(2) 6		(10) 12	
(3) 7		(11) 10	
(4) 9		(12) 8	
(5) 11		(13) 12	
(6) 6		(14) 14	
(7) 8		(15) 11	
(8) 6		(16) 13	

3

(1) 8		(7) 11	
(2) 11		(8) 13	
(3) 15		(9) 15	
(4) 11		(10) 13	
(5) 15		(11) 14	
(6) 13		(12) 17	

4

(1) 11		(9) 11	
(2) 10		(10) 13	
(3) 11		(11) 14	
(4) 15		(12) 11	
(5) 16		(13) 10	
(6) 13		(14) 18	
(7) 11		(15) 13	
(8) 12		(16) 4	

5 Review ◆Adding 7 to Adding 9 · pp 10,11

1

(1) 13		(14) 13	
(2) 9		(15) 16	
(3) 11		(16) 15	
(4) 14		(17) 11	
(5) 16		(18) 13	
(6) 15		(19) 16	
(7) 12		(20) 18	
(8) 10		(21) 17	
(9) 11		(22) 12	
(10) 14		(23) 14	
(11) 10		(24) 5	
(12) 9		(25) 0	
(13) 12			

2

(1) 12		(14) 10	
(2) 10		(15) 11	
(3) 12		(16) 11	
(4) 14		(17) 9	
(5) 13		(18) 17	
(6) 16		(19) 5	
(7) 15		(20) 12	
(8) 11		(21) 10	
(9) 12		(22) 8	
(10) 13		(23) 13	
(11) 12		(24) 0	
(12) 13		(25) 18	
(13) 14			

Advice

If you scored over 85 on this section, review your mistakes and move on to the next section.

If you scored between 75 and 84 on this section, review your addition a little more before continuing.

If you scored less than 74 on this section, it might be a good idea to go back to our "Grade 1 Addition" book and do an extended review of addition.

Advice

How many mistakes did you make? If you made a lot, try practicing your addition a little more.

6 Addition Review · pp 12,13

1

51	52	53	54	55	56	57	58	59	60
61	62	63	64	65	66	67	68	69	70
71	72	73	74	75	76	77	78	79	80
81	82	83	84	85	86	87	88	89	90
91	92	93	94	95	96	97	98	99	100

7 Subtracting 1 ◆2−1 to 11−1 · pp 14,15

1 | 1 | 2 | 3 | 4 | 5 | 6 | 7 | 8 | 9 | 10 |

2 | 10 | 9 | 8 | 7 | 6 | 5 | 4 | 3 | 2 | 1 |

3
(1) | 10 | 9 | 8 | 7 | 6 | 5 | 4 | 3 | 2 | 1 |
(2) | 10 | 9 | 8 | 7 | 6 | 5 |
(3) | 8 | 7 | 6 | 5 | 4 | 3 |
(4) | 6 | 5 | 4 | 3 | 2 | 1 |
(5) | 9 | 8 | 7 | 6 | 5 | 4 |
(6) | 7 | 6 | 5 | 4 | 3 | 2 |
(7) | 6 | 5 | 4 | 3 | 2 | 1 |

4
(1)	1	(6)	6
(2)	2	(7)	7
(3)	3	(8)	8
(4)	4	(9)	9
(5)	5	(10)	10

5
(1)	1	(7)	7
(2)	2	(8)	8
(3)	4	(9)	9
(4)	3	(10)	10
(5)	6	(11)	2
(6)	5	(12)	3

---

8 Subtracting 1 ◆2−1 to 11−1   pp 16, 17

1
(1)	1	(6)	8
(2)	2	(7)	9
(3)	3	(8)	10
(4)	6	(9)	4
(5)	7	(10)	5

2
(1)	7	(6)	5
(2)	8	(7)	6
(3)	9	(8)	1
(4)	10	(9)	2
(5)	4	(10)	3

3
(1)	1	(11)	5
(2)	3	(12)	7
(3)	5	(13)	9
(4)	7	(14)	4
(5)	9	(15)	6
(6)	2	(16)	8
(7)	4	(17)	10
(8)	6	(18)	3
(9)	8	(19)	2
(10)	10	(20)	4

---

9 Subtracting 1 ◆2−1 to 11−1   pp 18, 19

1
(1)	5	(6)	8
(2)	7	(7)	10
(3)	9	(8)	6
(4)	4	(9)	4
(5)	6	(10)	2

2
(1)	3	(6)	8
(2)	2	(7)	7
(3)	1	(8)	6
(4)	10	(9)	5
(5)	9	(10)	4

3
(1)	3	(11)	8
(2)	7	(12)	2
(3)	2	(13)	4
(4)	5	(14)	3
(5)	10	(15)	1
(6)	4	(16)	7
(7)	9	(17)	6
(8)	1	(18)	10
(9)	3	(19)	9
(10)	6	(20)	8

---

10 Subtracting 1 ◆2−1 to 14−1   pp 20, 21

1 | 1 | 2 | 3 | 4 | 5 | 6 | 7 | 8 | 9 | 10 | 11 | 12 | 13 | 14 |

2 | 14 | 13 | 12 | 11 | 10 | 9 | 8 | 7 | 6 | 5 | 4 | 3 | 2 | 1 |

3
(1) | 14 | 13 | 12 | 11 | 10 | 9 |
(2) | 12 | 11 | 10 | 9 | 8 | 7 |
(3) | 10 | 9 | 8 | 7 | 6 | 5 |
(4) | 8 | 7 | 6 | 5 | 4 | 3 |
(5) | 6 | 5 | 4 | 3 | 2 | 1 |
(6) | 13 | 12 | 11 | 10 | 9 | 8 |
(7) | 11 | 10 | 9 | 8 | 7 | 6 |
(8) | 9 | 8 | 7 | 6 | 5 | 4 |
(9) | 7 | 6 | 5 | 4 | 3 | 2 |
(10) | 6 | 5 | 4 | 3 | 2 | 1 |

4
(1)	4	(6)	9
(2)	5	(7)	10
(3)	6	(8)	11
(4)	7	(9)	12
(5)	8	(10)	13

5
(1)	7	(6)	11
(2)	8	(7)	12
(3)	1	(8)	13
(4)	2	(9)	9
(5)	3	(10)	10

---

11 Subtracting 1 ◆2−1 to 14−1   pp 22, 23

1
(1)	7	(11)	1
(2)	8	(12)	11
(3)	9	(13)	2
(4)	10	(14)	12
(5)	1	(15)	3
(6)	2	(16)	13
(7)	3	(17)	4
(8)	11	(18)	5
(9)	12	(19)	6
(10)	13	(20)	7

2
(1)	2	(11)	11
(2)	6	(12)	8
(3)	3	(13)	3
(4)	7	(14)	10
(5)	11	(15)	7
(6)	4	(16)	2
(7)	8	(17)	13
(8)	12	(18)	9
(9)	1	(19)	5
(10)	10	(20)	12

Advice

Did you manage to complete "Subtracting 1" easily and without many mistakes? Practice this repeatedly until you can!

12 Subtracting 2 ◆3−2 to 12−2 pp 24,25

1
(1) 1	(6) 6		
(2) 2	(7) 7		
(3) 3	(8) 8		
(4) 4	(9) 9		
(5) 5	(10) 10		

3
(1) 4	(6) 2
(2) 5	(7) 3
(3) 6	(8) 8
(4) 7	(9) 9
(5) 1	(10) 10

2
(1) 1	(6) 8
(2) 2	(7) 9
(3) 7	(8) 10
(4) 6	(9) 3
(5) 5	(10) 4

4
(1) 7	(6) 5
(2) 8	(7) 6
(3) 9	(8) 1
(4) 10	(9) 2
(5) 4	(10) 3

13 Subtracting 2 ◆3−2 to 12−2 pp 26,27

1
(1) 1	(6) 6
(2) 3	(7) 8
(3) 5	(8) 10
(4) 2	(9) 7
(5) 4	(10) 9

3
(1) 1	(11) 4
(2) 5	(12) 6
(3) 2	(13) 1
(4) 8	(14) 2
(5) 7	(15) 10
(6) 9	(16) 8
(7) 10	(17) 4
(8) 4	(18) 6
(9) 2	(19) 7
(10) 3	(20) 9

2
(1) 3	(6) 8
(2) 2	(7) 7
(3) 1	(8) 6
(4) 10	(9) 5
(5) 9	(10) 4

14 Subtracting 2 ◆3−2 to 15−2 pp 28,29

1
(1) 4	(6) 9
(2) 5	(7) 10
(3) 6	(8) 11
(4) 7	(9) 12
(5) 8	(10) 13

3
(1) 2	(11) 11
(2) 5	(12) 1
(3) 8	(13) 13
(4) 3	(14) 7
(5) 6	(15) 12
(6) 9	(16) 4
(7) 4	(17) 10
(8) 7	(18) 8
(9) 12	(19) 6
(10) 10	(20) 9

2
(1) 7	(6) 11
(2) 8	(7) 12
(3) 1	(8) 13
(4) 2	(9) 9
(5) 3	(10) 10

15 Subtracting 3 ◆4−3 to 13−3 pp 30,31

1
(1) 1	(6) 6
(2) 2	(7) 7
(3) 3	(8) 8
(4) 4	(9) 9
(5) 5	(10) 10

3
(1) 4	(6) 2
(2) 5	(7) 3
(3) 6	(8) 8
(4) 7	(9) 9
(5) 1	(10) 10

2
(1) 1	(6) 8
(2) 2	(7) 9
(3) 7	(8) 10
(4) 6	(9) 3
(5) 5	(10) 4

4
(1) 7	(6) 5
(2) 8	(7) 6
(3) 9	(8) 1
(4) 10	(9) 2
(5) 4	(10) 3

16 Subtracting 3 ◆4−3 to 13−3 pp 32,33

1
(1) 1	(6) 6
(2) 3	(7) 8
(3) 5	(8) 10
(4) 2	(9) 7
(5) 4	(10) 9

3
(1) 2	(11) 3
(2) 1	(12) 10
(3) 3	(13) 2
(4) 6	(14) 7
(5) 4	(15) 9
(6) 7	(16) 1
(7) 5	(17) 4
(8) 8	(18) 6
(9) 10	(19) 5
(10) 9	(20) 8

2
(1) 3	(6) 8
(2) 2	(7) 7
(3) 1	(8) 6
(4) 10	(9) 5
(5) 9	(10) 4

17 Subtracting 3 ◆3−3 to 16−3 pp 34,35

1
(1) 4	(6) 9
(2) 5	(7) 10
(3) 6	(8) 11
(4) 7	(9) 12
(5) 8	(10) 13

3
(1) 4	(11) 3
(2) 7	(12) 5
(3) 1	(13) 11
(4) 3	(14) 13
(5) 5	(15) 7
(6) 8	(16) 4
(7) 2	(17) 12
(8) 9	(18) 10
(9) 6	(19) 1
(10) 10	(20) 0

2
(1) 4	(6) 11
(2) 6	(7) 12
(3) 1	(8) 13
(4) 2	(9) 9
(5) 3	(10) 10

Advice

Did you make a lot of mistakes? If so, try a little extra review.

18 Subtracting 4 ◆5−4 to 14−4 pp 36,37

1
(1) 3	(11) 2		
(2) 2	(12) 5		
(3) 1	(13) 4		
(4) 4	(14) 3		
(5) 3	(15) 6		
(6) 2	(16) 5		
(7) 1	(17) 4		
(8) 5	(18) 8		
(9) 4	(19) 7		
(10) 3	(20) 6		

2
(1) 1	(6) 6
(2) 2	(7) 7
(3) 3	(8) 8
(4) 4	(9) 9
(5) 5	(10) 10

3
(1) 1	(6) 8
(2) 2	(7) 9
(3) 7	(8) 10
(4) 6	(9) 3
(5) 5	(10) 4

19 Subtracting 4 ◆4−4 to 17−4 pp 38,39

1
(1) 0	(6) 1
(2) 2	(7) 3
(3) 4	(8) 5
(4) 6	(9) 7
(5) 8	(10) 9

2
(1) 4	(6) 3
(2) 1	(7) 9
(3) 6	(8) 7
(4) 5	(9) 10
(5) 8	(10) 2

3
(1) 4	(6) 9
(2) 5	(7) 10
(3) 6	(8) 11
(4) 7	(9) 12
(5) 8	(10) 13

4
(1) 2	(6) 6
(2) 5	(7) 0
(3) 8	(8) 4
(4) 11	(9) 12
(5) 3	(10) 7

20 Subtracting 4 ◆4−4 to 17−4 pp 40,41

1
(1) 1	(11) 4
(2) 0	(12) 3
(3) 6	(13) 8
(4) 13	(14) 11
(5) 12	(15) 9
(6) 7	(16) 6
(7) 5	(17) 2
(8) 8	(18) 10
(9) 2	(19) 7
(10) 9	(20) 12

2
(1) 7	(11) 4
(2) 4	(12) 6
(3) 12	(13) 12
(4) 8	(14) 7
(5) 6	(15) 11
(6) 7	(16) 5
(7) 11	(17) 12
(8) 5	(18) 7
(9) 12	(19) 11
(10) 8	(20) 8

21 Subtracting 5 ◆6−5 to 15−5 pp 42,43

1
(1) 4	(11) 4
(2) 3	(12) 3
(3) 2	(13) 7
(4) 1	(14) 6
(5) 5	(15) 5
(6) 4	(16) 4
(7) 3	(17) 8
(8) 2	(18) 7
(9) 6	(19) 6
(10) 5	(20) 5

2
(1) 1	(6) 6
(2) 2	(7) 7
(3) 3	(8) 8
(4) 4	(9) 9
(5) 5	(10) 10

3
(1) 1	(6) 8
(2) 2	(7) 9
(3) 7	(8) 10
(4) 6	(9) 4
(5) 5	(10) 3

22 Subtracting 5 ◆5−5 to 18−5 pp 44,45

1
(1) 0	(6) 1
(2) 2	(7) 3
(3) 4	(8) 5
(4) 6	(9) 7
(5) 8	(10) 9

2
(1) 3	(6) 8
(2) 1	(7) 2
(3) 9	(8) 5
(4) 4	(9) 10
(5) 6	(10) 7

3
(1) 4	(6) 9
(2) 5	(7) 10
(3) 6	(8) 11
(4) 7	(9) 12
(5) 8	(10) 13

4
(1) 2	(6) 4
(2) 5	(7) 1
(3) 9	(8) 3
(4) 11	(9) 13
(5) 3	(10) 10

23 Subtracting 5 ◆5−5 to 18−5 pp 46,47

1
(1) 2	(11) 11
(2) 6	(12) 12
(3) 1	(13) 8
(4) 11	(14) 4
(5) 7	(15) 13
(6) 3	(16) 0
(7) 5	(17) 9
(8) 10	(18) 6
(9) 12	(19) 3
(10) 9	(20) 7

2
(1) 6	(11) 9
(2) 4	(12) 12
(3) 10	(13) 4
(4) 8	(14) 6
(5) 2	(15) 9
(6) 6	(16) 3
(7) 12	(17) 4
(8) 9	(18) 7
(9) 2	(19) 11
(10) 6	(20) 8

24 Subtraction
pp 48,49

1
(1) 3	(6) 2		
(2) 2	(7) 1		
(3) 1	(8) 4		
(4) 4	(9) 3		
(5) 3	(10) 2		

2
(1) 5	(6) 6
(2) 4	(7) 5
(3) 3	(8) 4
(4) 2	(9) 3
(5) 1	(10) 2

3
(1) 7	(6) 8
(2) 6	(7) 7
(3) 5	(8) 6
(4) 4	(9) 5
(5) 3	(10) 4

4
(1) 3	(6) 3
(2) 1	(7) 6
(3) 4	(8) 4
(4) 2	(9) 4
(5) 3	(10) 5

25 Subtraction
pp 50,51

1
(1) 4	(11) 4
(2) 2	(12) 5
(3) 1	(13) 3
(4) 3	(14) 2
(5) 4	(15) 1
(6) 5	(16) 5
(7) 3	(17) 4
(8) 2	(18) 3
(9) 1	(19) 2
(10) 6	(20) 1

2
(1) 2	(11) 0
(2) 0	(12) 1
(3) 5	(13) 3
(4) 2	(14) 2
(5) 4	(15) 5
(6) 1	(16) 8
(7) 4	(17) 5
(8) 5	(18) 3
(9) 3	(19) 7
(10) 2	(20) 4

26 Subtracting ◆From Numbers up to 10
pp 52,53

1
(1) 3	(14) 5
(2) 4	(15) 6
(3) 2	(16) 4
(4) 1	(17) 3
(5) 4	(18) 2
(6) 3	(19) 1
(7) 2	(20) 7
(8) 1	(21) 8
(9) 5	(22) 5
(10) 4	(23) 4
(11) 3	(24) 3
(12) 2	(25) 2
(13) 1	

2
(1) 2	(14) 6
(2) 0	(15) 0
(3) 2	(16) 3
(4) 1	(17) 7
(5) 0	(18) 3
(6) 4	(19) 5
(7) 2	(20) 6
(8) 0	(21) 4
(9) 1	(22) 8
(10) 4	(23) 0
(11) 2	(24) 2
(12) 0	(25) 1
(13) 1	

Advice

How did you do in that section? If it was tough, try a little more review.

27 Subtracting ◆From Numbers up to 11
pp 54,55

1
(1) 8	(14) 4
(2) 9	(15) 5
(3) 10	(16) 2
(4) 8	(17) 3
(5) 9	(18) 4
(6) 7	(19) 1
(7) 8	(20) 2
(8) 6	(21) 3
(9) 7	(22) 1
(10) 4	(23) 2
(11) 5	(24) 0
(12) 6	(25) 1
(13) 3	

2
(1) 6	(14) 6
(2) 7	(15) 3
(3) 8	(16) 6
(4) 5	(17) 3
(5) 6	(18) 9
(6) 2	(19) 5
(7) 3	(20) 2
(8) 4	(21) 7
(9) 0	(22) 4
(10) 1	(23) 8
(11) 2	(24) 0
(12) 0	(25) 1
(13) 0	

28 Subtracting ◆From Numbers up to 12
pp 56,57

1
(1) 9	(14) 4
(2) 10	(15) 5
(3) 11	(16) 2
(4) 9	(17) 3
(5) 10	(18) 4
(6) 8	(19) 1
(7) 9	(20) 2
(8) 7	(21) 3
(9) 8	(22) 1
(10) 6	(23) 2
(11) 7	(24) 0
(12) 5	(25) 1
(13) 6	

2
(1) 5	(14) 10
(2) 6	(15) 1
(3) 2	(16) 4
(4) 3	(17) 6
(5) 1	(18) 9
(6) 2	(19) 2
(7) 0	(20) 8
(8) 1	(21) 3
(9) 0	(22) 0
(10) 12	(23) 7
(11) 2	(24) 11
(12) 0	(25) 5
(13) 10	

29 Subtracting ◆From Numbers up to 13
pp 58,59

1

#	Ans	#	Ans
(1)	9	(14)	6
(2)	12	(15)	4
(3)	8	(16)	5
(4)	11	(17)	3
(5)	7	(18)	4
(6)	10	(19)	2
(7)	6	(20)	3
(8)	9	(21)	1
(9)	5	(22)	2
(10)	8	(23)	0
(11)	4	(24)	1
(12)	7	(25)	0
(13)	4		

2

#	Ans	#	Ans
(1)	8	(14)	10
(2)	10	(15)	7
(3)	6	(16)	2
(4)	8	(17)	5
(5)	3	(18)	13
(6)	5	(19)	6
(7)	2	(20)	3
(8)	4	(21)	8
(9)	0	(22)	0
(10)	0	(23)	9
(11)	12	(24)	4
(12)	0	(25)	1
(13)	13		

30 Subtracting ◆From Numbers up to 14
pp 60,61

1

#	Ans	#	Ans
(1)	9	(14)	7
(2)	13	(15)	2
(3)	8	(16)	6
(4)	12	(17)	1
(5)	7	(18)	5
(6)	11	(19)	0
(7)	6	(20)	4
(8)	10	(21)	1
(9)	5	(22)	3
(10)	9	(23)	0
(11)	4	(24)	2
(12)	8	(25)	1
(13)	3		

2

#	Ans	#	Ans
(1)	2	(14)	12
(2)	3	(15)	4
(3)	6	(16)	11
(4)	2	(17)	7
(5)	5	(18)	10
(6)	0	(19)	3
(7)	3	(20)	6
(8)	1	(21)	9
(9)	2	(22)	14
(10)	0	(23)	8
(11)	1	(24)	5
(12)	0	(25)	1
(13)	14		

31 Subtracting ◆From Numbers up to 15
pp 62,63

1

#	Ans	#	Ans
(1)	9	(14)	8
(2)	14	(15)	4
(3)	8	(16)	7
(4)	13	(17)	3
(5)	7	(18)	6
(6)	12	(19)	2
(7)	6	(20)	5
(8)	11	(21)	1
(9)	5	(22)	4
(10)	10	(23)	2
(11)	4	(24)	3
(12)	9	(25)	2
(13)	3		

2

#	Ans	#	Ans
(1)	6	(14)	12
(2)	8	(15)	2
(3)	4	(16)	6
(4)	6	(17)	9
(5)	1	(18)	4
(6)	3	(19)	15
(7)	1	(20)	11
(8)	2	(21)	5
(9)	0	(22)	8
(10)	1	(23)	1
(11)	0	(24)	7
(12)	15	(25)	3
(13)	5		

32 Subtracting ◆From Numbers up to 16
pp 64,65

1

#	Ans	#	Ans
(1)	6	(14)	7
(2)	3	(15)	2
(3)	2	(16)	5
(4)	9	(17)	6
(5)	6	(18)	4
(6)	8	(19)	3
(7)	4	(20)	15
(8)	7	(21)	14
(9)	11	(22)	13
(10)	3	(23)	12
(11)	9	(24)	11
(12)	13	(25)	10
(13)	2		

2

#	Ans	#	Ans
(1)	14	(14)	6
(2)	12	(15)	12
(3)	10	(16)	4
(4)	9	(17)	13
(5)	8	(18)	3
(6)	7	(19)	16
(7)	6	(20)	0
(8)	4	(21)	7
(9)	2	(22)	11
(10)	0	(23)	4
(11)	5	(24)	8
(12)	3	(25)	5
(13)	1		

33 Subtracting ◆From Numbers up to 17
pp 66,67

1

#	Ans	#	Ans
(1)	8	(14)	14
(2)	4	(15)	13
(3)	7	(16)	12
(4)	6	(17)	9
(5)	8	(18)	11
(6)	6	(19)	14
(7)	10	(20)	13
(8)	8	(21)	12
(9)	6	(22)	11
(10)	11	(23)	10
(11)	8	(24)	9
(12)	4	(25)	8
(13)	2		

2

#	Ans	#	Ans
(1)	9	(14)	10
(2)	11	(15)	7
(3)	12	(16)	11
(4)	10	(17)	2
(5)	8	(18)	6
(6)	6	(19)	9
(7)	4	(20)	3
(8)	2	(21)	8
(9)	0	(22)	5
(10)	7	(23)	12
(11)	5	(24)	0
(12)	3	(25)	17
(13)	1		

34 Subtracting ◆From Numbers up to 18
pp 68,69

1

#	Ans	#	Ans
(1)	6	(14)	10
(2)	9	(15)	5
(3)	2	(16)	9
(4)	8	(17)	3
(5)	5	(18)	8
(6)	1	(19)	15
(7)	9	(20)	14
(8)	6	(21)	13
(9)	14	(22)	12
(10)	10	(23)	11
(11)	5	(24)	10
(12)	7	(25)	9
(13)	0		

2

#	Ans	#	Ans
(1)	9	(14)	12
(2)	11	(15)	6
(3)	12	(16)	14
(4)	10	(17)	7
(5)	8	(18)	4
(6)	6	(19)	16
(7)	4	(20)	5
(8)	2	(21)	18
(9)	0	(22)	9
(10)	7	(23)	0
(11)	5	(24)	17
(12)	3	(25)	1
(13)	1		

35 Subtracting ◆From Numbers up to 19 pp 70,71

1

(1) 10	(14) 10
(2) 3	(15) 4
(3) 9	(16) 9
(4) 6	(17) 7
(5) 4	(18) 2
(6) 2	(19) 16
(7) 7	(20) 15
(8) 7	(21) 14
(9) 1	(22) 13
(10) 4	(23) 12
(11) 9	(24) 11
(12) 3	(25) 10
(13) 13	

2

(1) 11	(14) 9
(2) 15	(15) 4
(3) 10	(16) 12
(4) 9	(17) 16
(5) 8	(18) 10
(6) 6	(19) 17
(7) 4	(20) 8
(8) 7	(21) 5
(9) 5	(22) 2
(10) 3	(23) 7
(11) 1	(24) 18
(12) 2	(25) 1
(13) 0	

36 Subtracting ◆From Numbers up to 20 pp 72,73

1

(1) 5	(14) 5
(2) 8	(15) 2
(3) 10	(16) 19
(4) 8	(17) 18
(5) 6	(18) 17
(6) 9	(19) 16
(7) 5	(20) 15
(8) 9	(21) 14
(9) 13	(22) 13
(10) 3	(23) 12
(11) 9	(24) 11
(12) 3	(25) 10
(13) 10	

2

(1) 15	(14) 9
(2) 5	(15) 17
(3) 16	(16) 7
(4) 6	(17) 18
(5) 14	(18) 8
(6) 4	(19) 10
(7) 13	(20) 0
(8) 3	(21) 20
(9) 11	(22) 0
(10) 1	(23) 19
(11) 12	(24) 6
(12) 2	(25) 0
(13) 19	

Advice

Was this easy for you?
Keep practicing until you can finish a page without any mistakes. Remember that when you are subtracting a 1-digit number from 20, the answer will be a 2-digit number.
Also, when you subtract zero from a number you subtract nothing.
The answer will be the same number!

37 Subtraction Review pp 74,75

1

(1) 2	(14) 2
(2) 11	(15) 2
(3) 0	(16) 2
(4) 6	(17) 14
(5) 6	(18) 1
(6) 4	(19) 2
(7) 1	(20) 6
(8) 8	(21) 5
(9) 2	(22) 1
(10) 1	(23) 8
(11) 1	(24) 12
(12) 11	(25) 8
(13) 5	

2

(1) 3	(14) 2
(2) 2	(15) 1
(3) 5	(16) 8
(4) 12	(17) 0
(5) 4	(18) 7
(6) 9	(19) 4
(7) 17	(20) 4
(8) 6	(21) 4
(9) 16	(22) 8
(10) 4	(23) 2
(11) 15	(24) 4
(12) 3	(25) 7
(13) 14	

38 Subtraction Review pp 76,77

1

(1) 8	(14) 4
(2) 10	(15) 4
(3) 16	(16) 8
(4) 9	(17) 2
(5) 8	(18) 4
(6) 7	(19) 7
(7) 12	(20) 8
(8) 4	(21) 10
(9) 4	(22) 16
(10) 1	(23) 10
(11) 12	(24) 9
(12) 7	(25) 2
(13) 4	

2

(1) 10	(14) 10
(2) 2	(15) 11
(3) 4	(16) 13
(4) 12	(17) 4
(5) 5	(18) 14
(6) 6	(19) 11
(7) 7	(20) 14
(8) 13	(21) 12
(9) 9	(22) 5
(10) 4	(23) 9
(11) 5	(24) 14
(12) 8	(25) 18
(13) 8	

39 Subtraction Review pp 78,79

1

(1) 16	(14) 12
(2) 7	(15) 11
(3) 11	(16) 7
(4) 9	(17) 6
(5) 13	(18) 17
(6) 6	(19) 3
(7) 7	(20) 13
(8) 5	(21) 14
(9) 10	(22) 8
(10) 4	(23) 14
(11) 2	(24) 1
(12) 7	(25) 2
(13) 6	

2

(1) 10	(14) 3
(2) 15	(15) 18
(3) 9	(16) 5
(4) 5	(17) 4
(5) 2	(18) 5
(6) 3	(19) 3
(7) 9	(20) 5
(8) 13	(21) 4
(9) 3	(22) 2
(10) 8	(23) 7
(11) 5	(24) 8
(12) 6	(25) 7
(13) 6	

40 Three One-Digit Numbers ◆Mixed Calculations pp 80, 81

1
(1) 6　(6) 9
(2) 8　(7) 10
(3) 10　(8) 10
(4) 7　(9) 13
(5) 10　(10) 12

2
(1) 3　(6) 4
(2) 3　(7) 4
(3) 3　(8) 2
(4) 2　(9) 9
(5) 4　(10) 8

3
(1) 9　(11) 5
(2) 7　(12) 2
(3) 9　(13) 4
(4) 9　(14) 7
(5) 11　(15) 6
(6) 7　(16) 1
(7) 14　(17) 3
(8) 10　(18) 1
(9) 10　(19) 3
(10) 12　(20) 7

41 Three One-Digit Numbers ◆Mixed Calculations pp 82, 83

1
(1) 6　(6) 4
(2) 3　(7) 6
(3) 3　(8) 5
(4) 1　(9) 7
(5) 5　(10) 5

2
(1) 6　(6) 8
(2) 3　(7) 8
(3) 5　(8) 8
(4) 6　(9) 9
(5) 8　(10) 12

3
(1) 1　(11) 8
(2) 3　(12) 6
(3) 5　(13) 5
(4) 10　(14) 7
(5) 6　(15) 9
(6) 2　(16) 11
(7) 7　(17) 6
(8) 6　(18) 8
(9) 1　(19) 10
(10) 7　(20) 12

42 Three One-Digit Numbers ◆Mixed Calculations pp 84, 85

1
(1) 7　(11) 7
(2) 11　(12) 8
(3) 12　(13) 9
(4) 3　(14) 2
(5) 2　(15) 6
(6) 2　(16) 5
(7) 6　(17) 12
(8) 3　(18) 3
(9) 6　(19) 6
(10) 6　(20) 8

2
(1) 13　(11) 6
(2) 13　(12) 13
(3) 3　(13) 7
(4) 5　(14) 4
(5) 3　(15) 9
(6) 5　(16) 15
(7) 9　(17) 3
(8) 9　(18) 5
(9) 13　(19) 9
(10) 5　(20) 7

43 Review pp 86, 87

1
(1) 3　(14) 9
(2) 3　(15) 9
(3) 7　(16) 8
(4) 6　(17) 0
(5) 3　(18) 2
(6) 0　(19) 5
(7) 5　(20) 1
(8) 8　(21) 4
(9) 9　(22) 4
(10) 4　(23) 3
(11) 2　(24) 6
(12) 5　(25) 9
(13) 4

2
(1) 4　(14) 4
(2) 4　(15) 7
(3) 2　(16) 2
(4) 6　(17) 6
(5) 5　(18) 8
(6) 2　(19) 6
(7) 6　(20) 0
(8) 8　(21) 3
(9) 5　(22) 9
(10) 9　(23) 9
(11) 9　(24) 9
(12) 5　(25) 2
(13) 1

Advice

If you made many mistakes in **1**, start reviewing on page 14.

If you made many mistakes in **2**, start reviewing on page 52.